W9-CDV-331

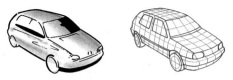    

THE USBORNE BOOK OF
CUTAWAY
CARS

Clive Gifford
Designed by Robert Walster

Consultant: Peter Cracknell
Series Editor: Cheryl Lanyon

Additional illustrations by Robert Walster, John Scorey and Sean Wilkinson.

Usborne Publishing wish to thank the following companies for their help with this book:

Citroën Ltd
Castrol International
Ford Motor Company Limited
Goodyear
Honda

Land Rover
Lotus
MIRA
Michelin Tyre PLC
Peugeot

Porsche Cars Great Britain Ltd
SAAB Automobile AB
Toyota
Volkswagen
Volvo

SCHOLASTIC INC.
New York Toronto London Auckland Sydney

Contents

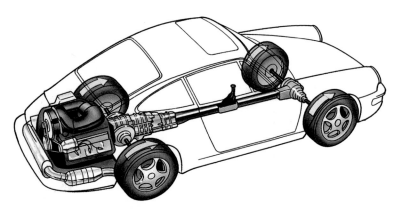

Words in *italic* type

Words which appear in *italic* type and are followed by a small star (for example, *friction**) can be found in the glossary on page 31.

Early cars

The first vehicle to move on land without the help of a horse or other animal was Nicolas-Joseph Cugnot's steam tractor. Built in 1769, it could only run for 15 minutes at a time and its top speed was just 3.6km/h (2.2mph), slower than you can walk.

Cugnot's steam tractor

This is its steam boiler.

This luxury car is a Delaunay-Belleville F6. It was first built in 1908 and was popular with nobles and aristocrats in Europe.

This hood opens out to protect the passengers sitting in the back seats.

These wheels were originally designed for cannons. They are made of wood and have spokes like bicycle wheels.

Here you can see the back axle, a rod which joins the back wheels together.

Most of the car's body is made of wood and is either painted or varnished. Car bodies today are usually made of steel.

The first big step in making cars more like they are today came with the invention of a new type of engine powered by gas or petrol. It was called the internal combustion engine and you can learn more about it on pages 10-11.

This Benz Velo was built in 1898.

One of the first cars to be powered by this new engine was built by Karl Benz in 1885. Within ten years, his factory was building many cars for sale. One model, the Benz Velo, was the first car to sell in large numbers.

As more companies started to build cars, improvements such as proper brakes and lights for driving at night were added. More powerful engines combined with better car design made cars much faster and this resulted in many more accidents. Governments brought in laws about cars and speed for the first time.

In Britain, until 1896, a person waving a red flag as a warning had to walk in front of a car. This kept speeds down to under 6.5km/h (4mph).

More reliable

The first motor vehicles were not reliable and broke down all the time. As cars became more popular, car builders concentrated on improving them so that they ran better. Rolls Royce built their first luxury car, the Silver Ghost, in 1906. To demonstrate its reliability, a team of drivers drove it non-stop for 24,120km (14,988 miles). In all this time, the car only had to stop once for repairs.

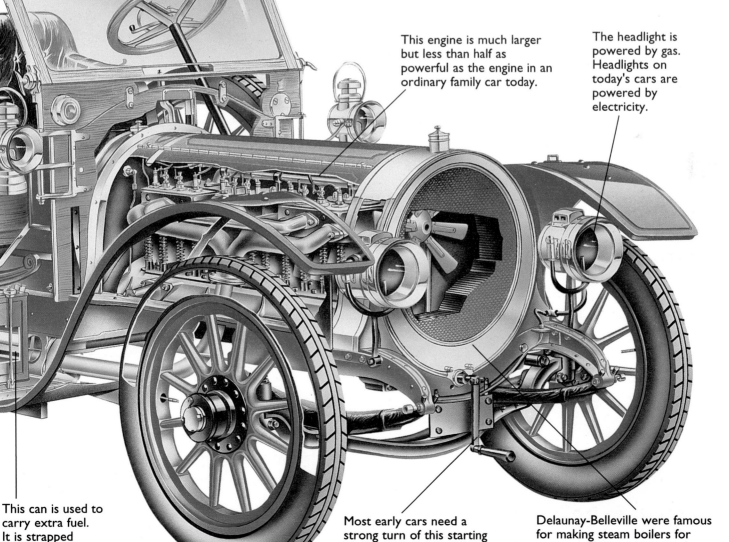

This windshield folds down.

This engine is much larger but less than half as powerful as the engine in an ordinary family car today.

The headlight is powered by gas. Headlights on today's cars are powered by electricity.

This can is used to carry extra fuel. It is strapped firmly into place.

Most early cars need a strong turn of this starting handle to start their engine up. A modern car uses electricity to start its engine.

Delaunay-Belleville were famous for making steam boilers for trains and ships. In fact, the shape of this engine cover is rather like a steam boiler.

Modern cars

An ordinary Volkswagen Golf

One hundred years on from the first motor vehicles, modern cars look a lot different. Yet, the way they work is, in fact, very similar. For example, most cars still rely on an internal combustion engine to power them. Today's cars are more complicated than earlier models. They are made up of hundreds of parts all joined together to form what car engineers call systems.

A Golf used for rally racing

From design to production

It takes many years to design and build a modern car. First, the company researches what customers want and finds out what are the latest technical developments. They then start to choose some of the basic features they wish to include in the new car.

A car starts its life as drawings on a designer's desk. Changes are suggested by many people in the company. Everything from the seat colour to the size of the wheels is discussed.

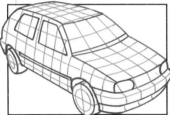

Engineers use Computer Aided Design (or C.A.D.) to determine the size and shape of the car and all its parts. Then, detailed plans and models of the car are made.

The models are tested in wind tunnels (see page 17) to see how they react to air moving over them. Many changes are made to the car's shape and testing lasts a long time.

Many other tests are done before the car can be produced in large numbers to sell to the public. Some of the most important testing is for safety (see pages 6-7).

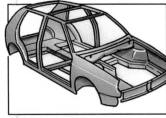

The parts of the car are made in several different factories. Some parts are even made by other companies. The car is then put together on a production line in a factory.

Eventually, cars come off the production line, are given a final test and are ready to be sold. The time between the original design and the first sales can be over five years.

Volkswagen Golf

The Volkswagen Golf is a popular family car. It is relatively small and compact but can carry up to five people and travel at speeds over 160km/h (100mph).

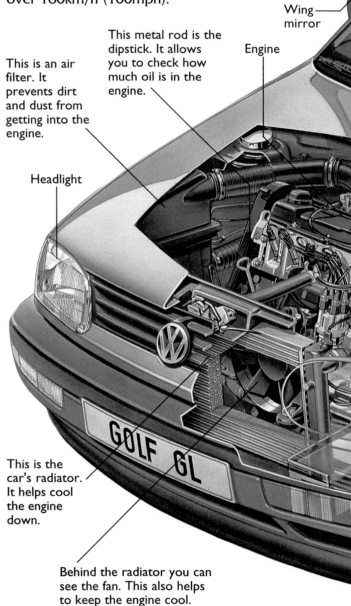

Wing mirror

This metal rod is the dipstick. It allows you to check how much oil is in the engine.

Engine

This is an air filter. It prevents dirt and dust from getting into the engine.

Headlight

This is the car's radiator. It helps cool the engine down.

Behind the radiator you can see the fan. This also helps to keep the engine cool.

Chassis and monocoque

The car's main parts used to be held in place by a frame called a *chassis**. Family cars today usually have a chassis combined with the body of the car. This is called a monocoque.

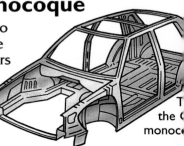

the
monoco

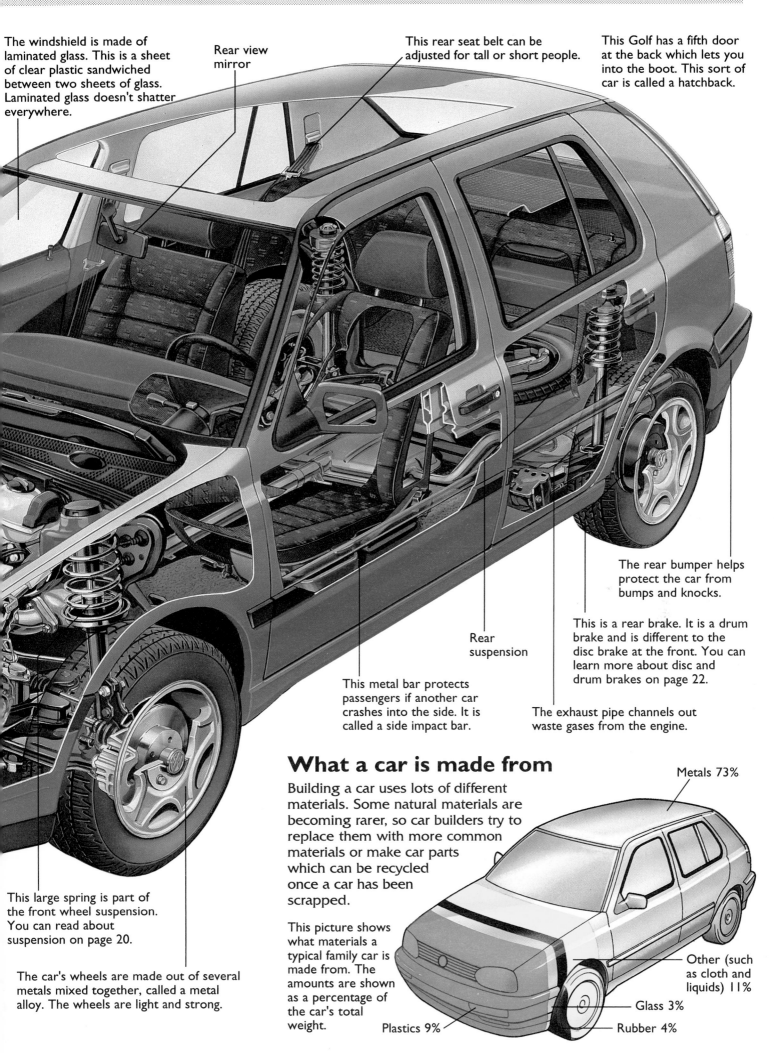

The windshield is made of laminated glass. This is a sheet of clear plastic sandwiched between two sheets of glass. Laminated glass doesn't shatter everywhere.

Rear view mirror

This rear seat belt can be adjusted for tall or short people.

This Golf has a fifth door at the back which lets you into the boot. This sort of car is called a hatchback.

The rear bumper helps protect the car from bumps and knocks.

This is a rear brake. It is a drum brake and is different to the disc brake at the front. You can learn more about disc and drum brakes on page 22.

Rear suspension

This metal bar protects passengers if another car crashes into the side. It is called a side impact bar.

The exhaust pipe channels out waste gases from the engine.

This large spring is part of the front wheel suspension. You can read about suspension on page 20.

The car's wheels are made out of several metals mixed together, called a metal alloy. The wheels are light and strong.

What a car is made from

Building a car uses lots of different materials. Some natural materials are becoming rarer, so car builders try to replace them with more common materials or make car parts which can be recycled once a car has been scrapped.

This picture shows what materials a typical family car is made from. The amounts are shown as a percentage of the car's total weight.

Metals 73%

Other (such as cloth and liquids) 11%

Glass 3%

Rubber 4%

Plastics 9%

Safety

Modern cars are designed to help the driver avoid accidents. The latest brakes, steering and tyres all give drivers more control of their car than ever before. These are called active safety features.

If there is an accident, a car's passive safety features protect the driver and passengers. The picture below shows some of the common passive safety features of a modern car in a crash test.

Dummies are used instead of people when a car is crash tested. Their movements and any damage they suffer is recorded using high speed photography and sensors linked to computers.

Crash test dummy

This is a steering wheel air bag (see how it works below).

To stop the driver's head from hitting the steering wheel, the steering column, to which the wheel is attached, can be made to collapse like a telescope.

This headrest stops the head from jolting sharply back. This action is called whiplash and can cause severe back and neck damage.

The seat is firmly fixed to the floor. It cannot slide back and trap the legs of a passenger in the back seat.

Seat belts hold people firmly in their seats. Many modern seat belts are fitted with powerful springs called pre-tensioners. They pull the belt tighter if there's a crash.

Submarining is when people are forced forward and under their seat belts by a crash. Modern seats are designed to stop this.

The front of the car body will crumple as the car hits something solid.

Steering wheel air bag

As a car hits something it starts to slow down and stop but the people inside the car keep moving. Many people in crashes are hurt by hitting their heads on the steering wheel or dashboard. An air bag should prevent this.

An air bag must inflate very quickly and stay blown-up until after the driver's head has hit it. This is done by igniting, or setting light to, chemicals which create large amounts of gases. These gases inflate the bag in an instant. Some cars have air bags to protect the front passenger as well.

Gases inflate air bag.

Inflating chemical is stored here.

Igniter sets light to chemicals to create gases.

Switches inside the car set off the chemicals in the air bag when the car crashes at over 33km/h (20mph).

The chemicals react and inflate the bag. A large cushion for the driver's chest and head is created.

The bag inflates in 40 milliseconds. That's less than a third of the time it takes you to blink your eye.

Body strength

Crashes create energy which has to go somewhere. Early car bodies were rigid. These protected against the direct impact of a crash only for the energy to travel through the car and throw people around.

A modern car still has a rigid body, called the passenger cell or cage, which will not break even if the car rolls over. Much of the rest of the car's body is designed to collapse when it is hit. The collapsing parts are called crumple zones and they absorb lots of energy from the crash. The remaining energy is directed around the car body but away from the driver and passengers.

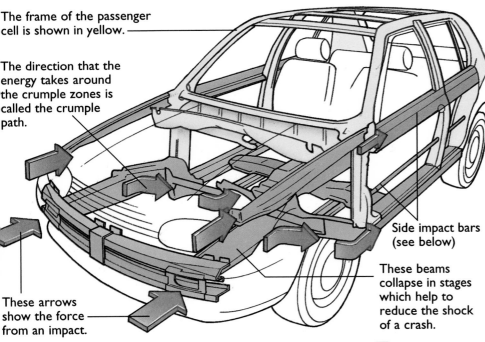

The frame of the passenger cell is shown in yellow.

The direction that the energy takes around the crumple zones is called the crumple path.

These arrows show the force from an impact.

Side impact bars (see below)

These beams collapse in stages which help to reduce the shock of a crash.

Side impact bars

Many accidents involve side-on crashes where one car punches a hole through another's door. Although some companies are starting to use side air bags, the most common way to protect people is to put strong rods of steel, called side impact bars, inside the door frame.

Side impact bars

Computer simulation

Some car companies use powerful computers to improve car safety. They build a model of the car in the computer which is accurate right down to the last detail.

Although this takes a long time to do, it allows every part of the car to be crash tested in the computer. Engineers can alter the size or the strength of a piece of the car at the touch of a few buttons, and see the effect more quickly than building a proper part which has to be checked in a real car crash test.

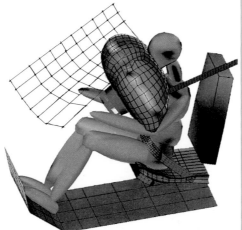

This is a computer test of the air bag opening.

The tests can take as long as 30 hours to complete but provide the safety team with lots of important information.

Crash testing

Crash tests have to cover all the different possible types of crash. Engineers record what happens to a car in each crash by using photography and electronic instruments, both inside and outside of the car. They can then tell what changes may be needed to improve the car's design.

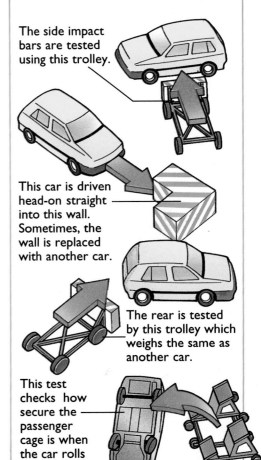

The side impact bars are tested using this trolley.

This car is driven head-on straight into this wall. Sometimes, the wall is replaced with another car.

The rear is tested by this trolley which weighs the same as another car.

This test checks how secure the passenger cage is when the car rolls over.

This is an overhead view of a crash test to the front of a car.

Rally car

Rally cars race in difficult conditions: through deserts, over icy roads and on bumpy dirt tracks, for example. They have to be tough to take the battering they receive. Most rally cars are specially modified versions of normal family cars.

Ford Escort RS Cosworth

This car has won a lot of competitions. It is based on a high speed version of the Ford Escort. It has many features added including a strengthened body, tougher, lighter wheels and a bigger, more powerful engine.

This is a standard Ford Escort.

Wings

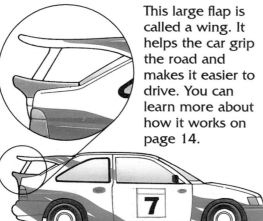

This large flap is called a wing. It helps the car grip the road and makes it easier to drive. You can learn more about how it works on page 14.

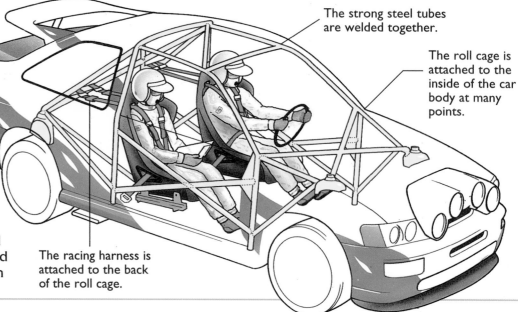

Rear wing

This car is fitted with studded tyres, used for driving on ice and snow.

This is the car's exhaust pipe. Its unusual flat shape stops it from hitting bumps in the ground.

These seats are specially shaped to hold the driver and co-driver. They are called bucket seats.

The co-driver sits here. He or she plots the car's route around the rally course.

Driver protection

Rally cars crash and roll over more often than family cars. In a rally car, the driver and co-driver are protected by a strong frame of steel tubes fitted to the inside of the car body. This frame is called a roll cage.

The driver and co-driver are held firmly in their seats by a set of five straps called a racing harness. These straps go around the waist, over the shoulders and between the legs. They all fasten together at the front.

The strong steel tubes are welded together.

The roll cage is attached to the inside of the car body at many points.

The racing harness is attached to the back of the roll cage.

The body is cut away here to show part of the roll cage (see below).

This roof vent lets air into the car.

Lights

The Escort Cosworth sometimes has four extra front lights for rallying at night or racing along tracks in dark forests. Each of these lights is about twice as strong as a normal car headlight.

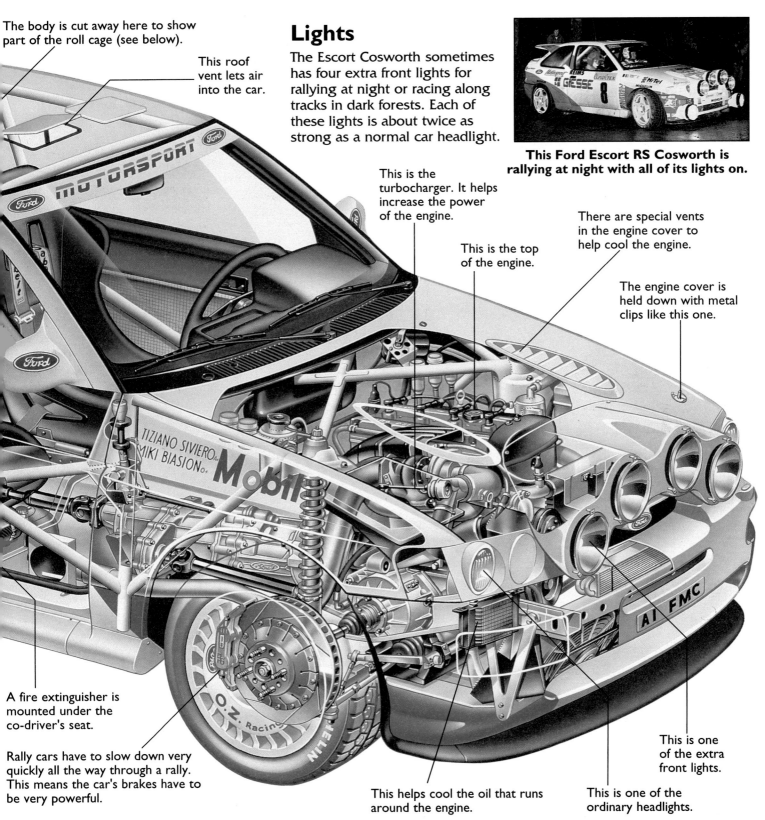

This Ford Escort RS Cosworth is rallying at night with all of its lights on.

This is the turbocharger. It helps increase the power of the engine.

This is the top of the engine.

There are special vents in the engine cover to help cool the engine.

The engine cover is held down with metal clips like this one.

A fire extinguisher is mounted under the co-driver's seat.

Rally cars have to slow down very quickly all the way through a rally. This means the car's brakes have to be very powerful.

This helps cool the oil that runs around the engine.

This is one of the ordinary headlights.

This is one of the extra front lights.

Rally racing

Rally courses are a mixture of roads and dirt tracks. The course is divided into separate sections known as Special Stages. One stage may be along twisting and turning mountain roads, another on mud tracks through dark forests. The cars follow the same route but start one after another. Each car is timed over the different stages by officials called marshals. The winner is the car which has the fastest overall time.

Cars at the bigger rallies are supported by teams of dozens of people and many vehicles. These can include motorcycles to carry messages, trucks holding spare parts, a medical van and, sometimes, even a helicopter.

This car, without extra lights, is racing along a twisting mountain road.

9

The engine

Most cars are powered by a type of engine called an internal combustion, or I.C., engine. It is called this because it produces power by combusting, or burning, a mixture of fuel and air inside a chamber called a cylinder.

How an I.C. engine works

Here are the names of many of the important parts at the heart of an I.C. engine.

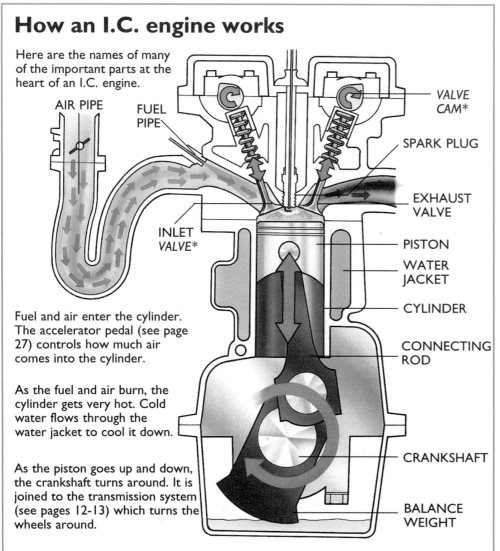

AIR PIPE

FUEL PIPE

VALVE CAM*

SPARK PLUG

EXHAUST VALVE

INLET VALVE*

PISTON

WATER JACKET

CYLINDER

CONNECTING ROD

CRANKSHAFT

BALANCE WEIGHT

Fuel and air enter the cylinder. The accelerator pedal (see page 27) controls how much air comes into the cylinder.

As the fuel and air burn, the cylinder gets very hot. Cold water flows through the water jacket to cool it down.

As the piston goes up and down, the crankshaft turns around. It is joined to the transmission system (see pages 12-13) which turns the wheels around.

The actions that create power in the cylinder are called the combustion cycle. Most car engines have a cycle of four strokes. This means that the piston moves up twice and down twice in one complete cycle.

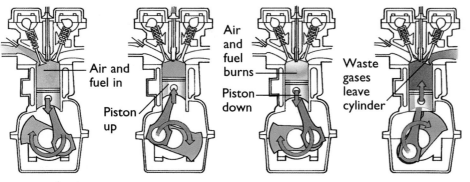

Air and fuel in

Piston up

Air and fuel burns

Piston down

Waste gases leave cylinder

1. At the cycle's start, the piston moves down and the inlet valve opens. The fuel and air mixture is sucked into the cylinder.

2. The piston moves up the cylinder. This compresses and heats up the fuel and air. The spark plug sets light to the mixture.

3. The mixture burns, creating gases which expand quickly. These push the piston down. This stroke produces the engine's power.

4. The exhaust valve opens and the waste gases are pushed out of the cylinder by the rising piston. The engine then starts another complete cycle.

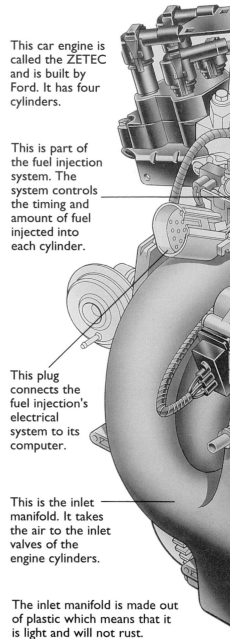

This car engine is called the ZETEC and is built by Ford. It has four cylinders.

This is part of the fuel injection system. The system controls the timing and amount of fuel injected into each cylinder.

This plug connects the fuel injection's electrical system to its computer.

This is the inlet manifold. It takes the air to the inlet valves of the engine cylinders.

The inlet manifold is made out of plastic which means that it is light and will not rust.

How many cylinders?

A modern car engine has more than one cylinder. A small engine may have four while engines used in powerful racing or sports cars can have as many as twelve. They can be arranged in different patterns.

This engine's four cylinders are arranged in line.

This engine's eight cylinders are arranged in a V pattern.

This combination is called a flat six.

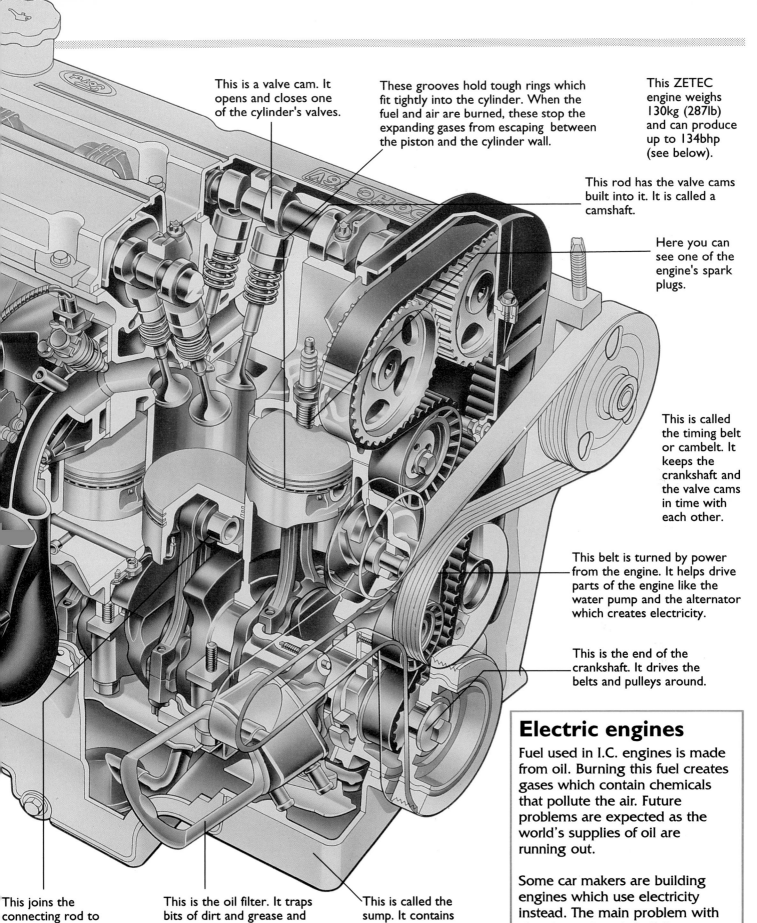

This is a valve cam. It opens and closes one of the cylinder's valves.

These grooves hold tough rings which fit tightly into the cylinder. When the fuel and air are burned, these stop the expanding gases from escaping between the piston and the cylinder wall.

This ZETEC engine weighs 130kg (287lb) and can produce up to 134bhp (see below).

This rod has the valve cams built into it. It is called a camshaft.

Here you can see one of the engine's spark plugs.

This is called the timing belt or cambelt. It keeps the crankshaft and the valve cams in time with each other.

This belt is turned by power from the engine. It helps drive parts of the engine like the water pump and the alternator which creates electricity.

This is the end of the crankshaft. It drives the belts and pulleys around.

This joins the connecting rod to the piston. It is called a gudgeon pin.

This is the oil filter. It traps bits of dirt and grease and stops them from going into the engine.

This is called the sump. It contains oil which acts as a *lubricant** as the engine runs.

Measuring power

The amount of power the engine can supply from the crankshaft is called its brake horsepower (bhp). This is the most common way of describing how powerful an internal combustion engine is. A modern small family car engine produces between 50 and 100bhp, while very powerful sports car engines can produce over 300bhp.

Electric engines

Fuel used in I.C. engines is made from oil. Burning this fuel creates gases which contain chemicals that pollute the air. Future problems are expected as the world's supplies of oil are running out.

Some car makers are building engines which use electricity instead. The main problem with electric engines is building efficient batteries which can store enough electricity to power a car.

This Japanese IZA electric car has a top speed of 176km/h (110mph).

11

The transmission

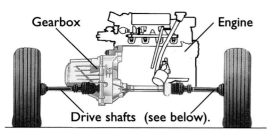

Gearbox — **Engine**

Drive shafts (see below).

The transmission system sends power from the engine to the wheels. The first transmissions were like bicycle chains, but in today's cars they are made up of many parts. A modern transmission passes the power from the engine through a gearbox, which gives the driver a chance to select different speeds.

The power is then taken to whicheve wheels push the car forward. Twenty years ago, most cars were powered by their rear wheels but today more and more cars have a transmission system which drives the front wheel like the one shown below. Some car are even driven by all four wheels (see page 24).

Gearbox

The heart of a transmission system is the gearbox. This system, made by Saab, has a gearbox with five forward gears and one reverse. Here you can see the names of some of its parts. The explanations on these two pages tell you how it all works.

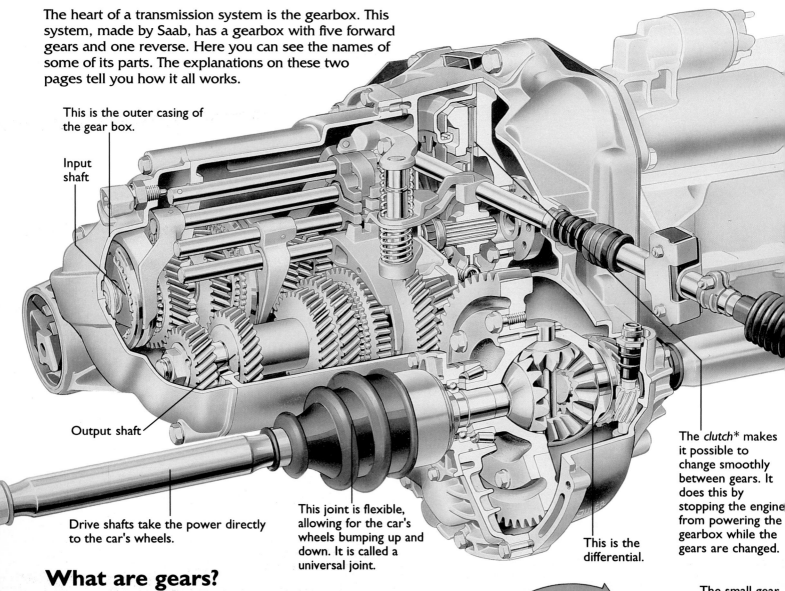

This is the outer casing of the gear box.

Input shaft

Output shaft

Drive shafts take the power directly to the car's wheels.

This joint is flexible, allowing for the car's wheels bumping up and down. It is called a universal joint.

This is the differential.

The *clutch** makes it possible to change smoothly between gears. It does this by stopping the engine from powering the gearbox while the gears are changed.

What are gears?

The gears found in a car gearbox are called cogs and are like wheels with teeth. The teeth allow gears to interlock, or mesh. When the gears mesh together, turning one gear around makes the other turn, but in the other direction.

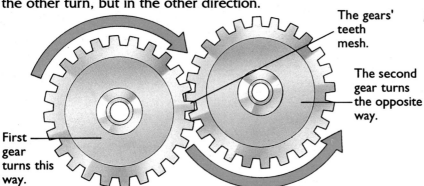

The gears' teeth mesh.

The second gear turns the opposite way.

First gear turns this way.

The small gear turns four time for each turn o the large.

Large gear four times bigger than small gear.

Large gear turns with four times more torque (see below) than the small gear.

If the gears are different sizes, the smaller one turns faster but the slower, bigger gear turns with greater power. Turning power is called *torque** by engineers and mechanics.

How the gearbox works

A car's gearbox contains many gear cogs which together provide the car with four, five or six different speeds. A car needs these because driving requires different combinations of speed and force at different times. For example, driving up a steep hill needs more force than speed while cruising along a motorway needs more speed than force. The lower gears in a gearbox provide greater force and the higher gears more speed.

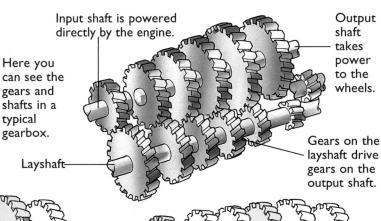

Input shaft is powered directly by the engine.

Here you can see the gears and shafts in a typical gearbox.

Output shaft takes power to the wheels.

Layshaft

Gears on the layshaft drive gears on the output shaft.

On top of the gear stick is this pattern showing where each gear is.

Gear stick

Gear shift rod

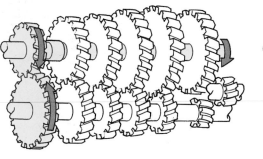

Layshaft

In first gear, a small wheel on the layshaft and a large wheel on the output shaft connect. The car moves slowly but with much power.

In second gear, the two gear cogs have less difference in size. This gear turns more quickly but with less power. This helps the car pull away with ease.

In the highest gear, the cogs on the input and output shafts are linked so that they turn at the same rate. This top gear allows the car to go at its fastest.

Output shaft turns opposite way to usual.

Idler gear

In reverse, an extra gear, called an idler gear, slips in between the normal input and output gears. The output shaft and the car's wheels turn the opposite way.

What is the differential?

The differential is a complicated set of gears between the two drive shafts of whichever wheels power the car. The differential adjusts the speed at which the two wheels turn when the car goes around a corner. The outer wheel has to travel farther around a corner than the inner one. The differential's gears make the outer wheel turn faster than the inner one.

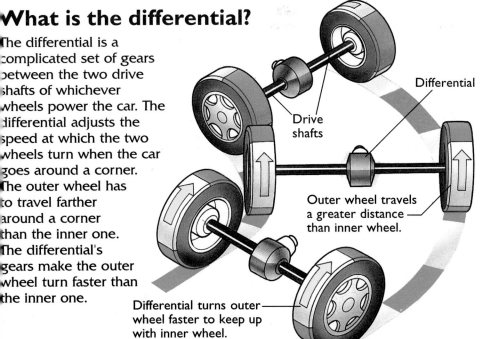

Differential

Drive shafts

Outer wheel travels a greater distance than inner wheel.

Differential turns outer wheel faster to keep up with inner wheel.

Automatic gearbox

Changing from one gear to another constantly can be tiring. One solution is an automatic gearbox that selects the engine gears for you. Automatic transmissions tend to use more fuel and the driver still has to make some choices by selecting with the gear stick.

P is for when the car is parked.

D is for drive, the main forward gear.

R is reverse gear.

Grand Prix racing car

Grand Prix racing is the most famous type of racing. With their powerful engines and light, specially-designed bodies, Grand Prix cars can travel at speeds of up to 320km/h (200mph). Grand Prix cars are often the first to use new technology. Some of the advanced features which prove useful for normal road drivers are eventually seen on ordinary family cars.

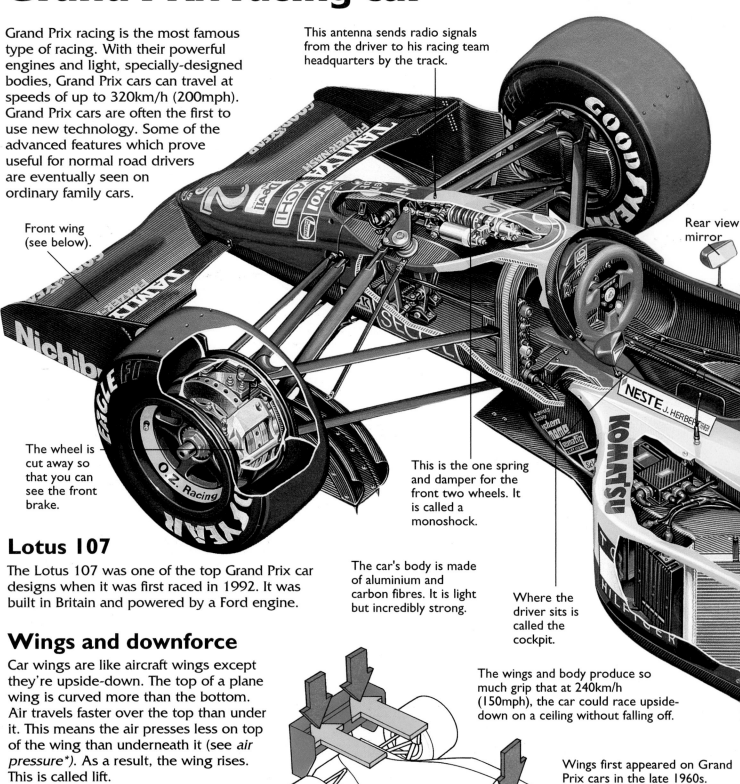

This antenna sends radio signals from the driver to his racing team headquarters by the track.

Front wing (see below).

Rear view mirror

The wheel is cut away so that you can see the front brake.

This is the one spring and damper for the front two wheels. It is called a monoshock.

Lotus 107

The Lotus 107 was one of the top Grand Prix car designs when it was first raced in 1992. It was built in Britain and powered by a Ford engine.

The car's body is made of aluminium and carbon fibres. It is light but incredibly strong.

Where the driver sits is called the cockpit.

Wings and downforce

Car wings are like aircraft wings except they're upside-down. The top of a plane wing is curved more than the bottom. Air travels faster over the top than under it. This means the air presses less on top of the wing than underneath it (see *air pressure**). As a result, the wing rises. This is called lift.

Air travels over wing.

Wing rises upwards.

Car wings do the opposite to plane wings. Instead of producing lift, they help the car stick to the ground. The force that makes a car grip the track is called downforce. It helps the car grip without slowing it down too much and gives the driver more control when turning.

The wings and body produce so much grip that at 240km/h (150mph), the car could race upside-down on a ceiling without falling off.

Wings first appeared on Grand Prix cars in the late 1960s.

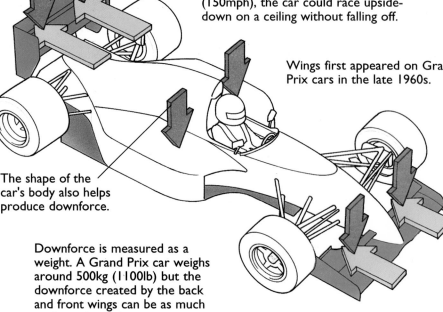

The shape of the car's body also helps produce downforce.

Downforce is measured as a weight. A Grand Prix car weighs around 500kg (1100lb) but the downforce created by the back and front wings can be as much as three times that.

14

Grand Prix engines

Grand Prix racing pushes a car, and especially the engine, to its absolute limits. Most engines are completely rebuilt after each race. The mechanics study the telemetrics, which are the performance details of the car recorded on computer during the race. They then rebuild and modify the engine according to the results.

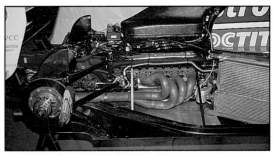

This is the Lotus 107 raced by British driver, Johnny Herbert.

This Ford Cosworth HB engine powers the Lotus 107 and is protected by an advanced lubricant made by its sponsor, Castrol.

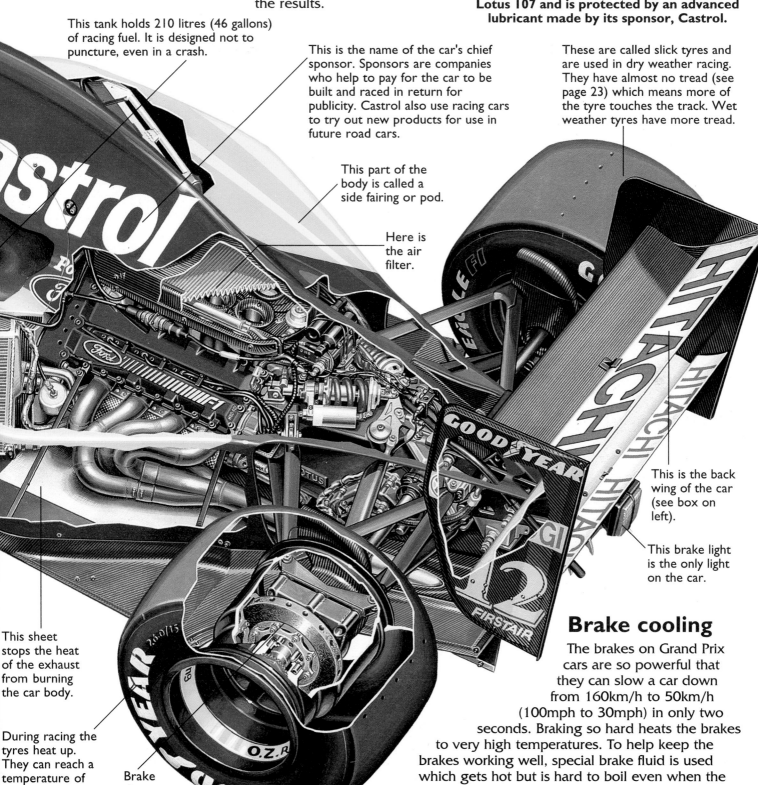

This tank holds 210 litres (46 gallons) of racing fuel. It is designed not to puncture, even in a crash.

This is the name of the car's chief sponsor. Sponsors are companies who help to pay for the car to be built and raced in return for publicity. Castrol also use racing cars to try out new products for use in future road cars.

This part of the body is called a side fairing or pod.

Here is the air filter.

These are called slick tyres and are used in dry weather racing. They have almost no tread (see page 23) which means more of the tyre touches the track. Wet weather tyres have more tread.

This is the back wing of the car (see box on left).

This brake light is the only light on the car.

This sheet stops the heat of the exhaust from burning the car body.

During racing the tyres heat up. They can reach a temperature of 110°C (230°F).

Brake disc

Brake cooling

The brakes on Grand Prix cars are so powerful that they can slow a car down from 160km/h to 50km/h (100mph to 30mph) in only two seconds. Braking so hard heats the brakes to very high temperatures. To help keep the brakes working well, special brake fluid is used which gets hot but is hard to boil even when the brakes are in constant use.

Aerodynamics

To understand aerodynamics, you need to know about friction. Friction is the scientific name for when two things rub together. You can feel the effects of friction if you rub your hands together.

The tighter you press your hands together the more effort it takes to move them. After a short while, your hands start to warm up. If you kept rubbing them for a long time, the friction would cause wear and you would get blisters.

Friction wastes power, creates heat and, over time, wears down the surfaces of objects rubbing together. Reducing friction means that cars can move faster and with less effort.

Without friction, a car wouldn't go at all. Friction between wheels and the ground allows the wheels to grip the ground and push the car forward. A car's brakes also rely on friction to slow the wheels down.

The tyres grip even when the car moves up a steep slope.

The friction of air

When air and a moving object rub together they create friction. Today's cars are designed to cause less air friction than cars in the past. Their particular shapes and some of their features were developed by the use of aerodynamics.

Aerodynamics is the study of how a moving object travels through the air. It was first developed to look at how aircraft fly but is now used on motor vehicles as well.

Modern cars have smooth, rounded shapes (known as *streamlined**) which air passes over easily. This reduces the amount of friction from the air.

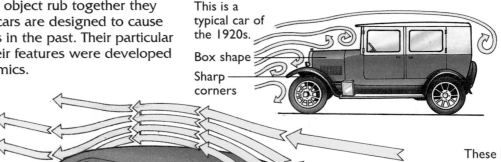

This is a typical car of the 1920s.

Box shape

Sharp corners

Air hits the front of the car flat on. The air cannot easily pass over and around the car so it creates lots of air friction.

These lines show the way air flows, or travels, over the car.

Streamlined features on cars

Wheel arches fit closely around the wheel.

Door handles fit flush into the car body.

The lights are moulded into the body of the car.

The windshield is angled back.

The wing mirrors are rounded and smooth.

Drag coefficient

The drag coefficient, or Cd, is a measure of how much air friction a particular car will encounter. Less air friction means the car uses less fuel. Drag coefficients have got smaller as cars have become more streamlined. A family car in the 1960s had a drag coefficient of around 0.5 or 0.45. In today's family car, it is around 0.3.

This Vesta research car, built by Renault, has a drag coefficient of only 0.1

Reducing friction

In a car, the surfaces of moving parts that rub together are made as smooth as possible to reduce friction. A liquid is far smoother than the surfaces of the car parts. A thin layer of liquid, usually oil, placed between the moving parts will produce a smoother surface and less friction. A liquid used in this way is called a *lubricant**.

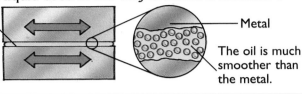

Thin layer of oil between two moving surfaces.

Metal

The oil is much smoother than the metal.

A rolling movement creates less friction than a sliding one. You can see this for yourself. First slide a book across a table. Then put some marbles underneath it and push it across the table again. The marbles roll rather than slide and this rolling creates less friction which means the book moves more easily. In some car parts, steel balls do the same job as the marbles.

These steel balls are called ball bearings.

Wind tunnel

One of the most important tools used in aerodynamics is a wind tunnel. It allows scientists to measure and record exactly how air travels around a car at different speeds. A modern wind tunnel can also mimic extreme weather to see how parts of the car react. For example, strong jets of water can mimic very heavy rain to see if the car has any tiny leaks.

This powerful fan can be adjusted to provide different strengths of wind.

Water can be injected into the air, to simulate rain or fog.

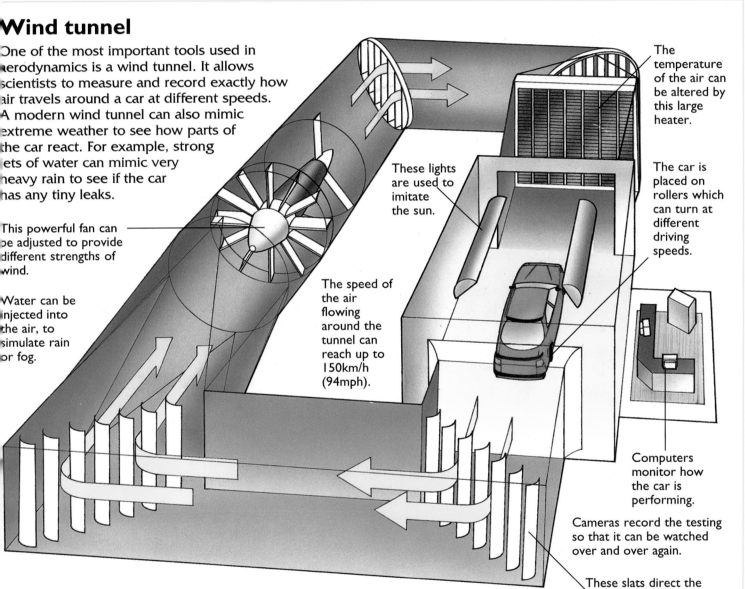

These lights are used to imitate the sun.

The speed of the air flowing around the tunnel can reach up to 150km/h (94mph).

The temperature of the air can be altered by this large heater.

The car is placed on rollers which can turn at different driving speeds.

Computers monitor how the car is performing.

Cameras record the testing so that it can be watched over and over again.

These slats direct the air around the tunnel.

Watching the flow of air

Air is invisible, but its journey over and around a car needs to be watched and recorded. So, engineers have had to invent special techniques to see the air.

This man is injecting white gas into the air just before it flows around the car. Engineers can then see how the air travels.

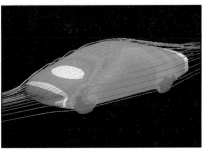

This computer is imitating the flow of air over a model car. Computers have greatly helped to improve cars' aerodynamics.

17

Vintage racing car

Almost as soon as cars were invented, they were raced against each other. The first official race was in France in 1895. In the early part of the twentieth century, cars built solely for racing first appeared. They competed in famous races such as the Mille Miglia in Italy and the 24 hour race in Le Mans in France. Many of the original cars have been restored and can be found in museums or even racing on tracks at vintage car rallies.

Bentley 4½ Litre

This famous vintage racing car was first built in 1930. Earlier versions of the car raced throughout the 1920s and won Le Mans every year between 1927 and 1930.

The name 4½ Litre refers to the *volume** of the engine's cylinders all added together. This measure is called cubic capacity and is measured in cubic centimetres or cc.

This is a Bentley 4½ Litre from the National Motor Museum in Beaulieu, England.

Le Mans today

The Le Mans race still takes place today but the cars racing in the competition have changed greatly since cars like the Bentley 4½ Litre raced there. For example, the first winning Bentley in 1927 raced at an average speed of 98km/h (61mph). The 1993 winner (shown right) raced at an average speed of 214km/h (132mph).

Modern light materials and a smaller but more powerful engine means that the Peugeot weighs just over a third of the weight of the Bentley so it goes faster. The Peugeot's top speed is over 400km/h (250mph). That is twice as fast as the Bentley.

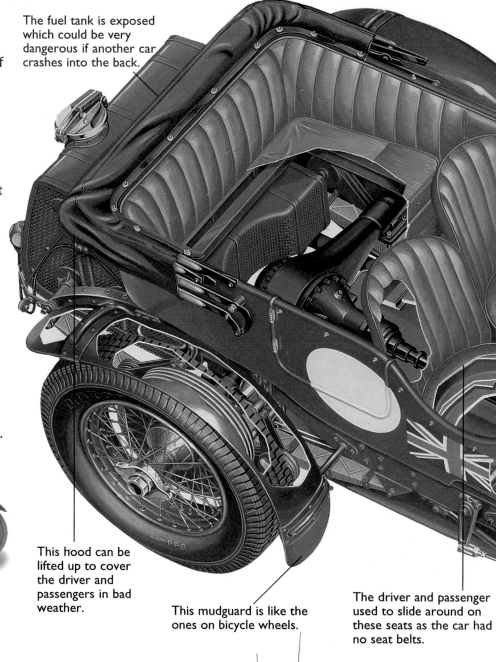

The fuel tank is exposed which could be very dangerous if another car crashes into the back.

This hood can be lifted up to cover the driver and passengers in bad weather.

This mudguard is like the ones on bicycle wheels.

The driver and passenger used to slide around on these seats as the car had no seat belts.

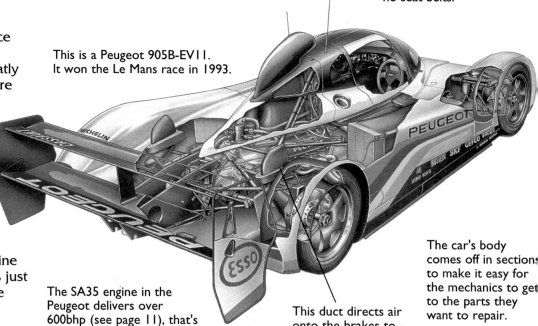

This is a Peugeot 905B-EV11. It won the Le Mans race in 1993.

The SA35 engine in the Peugeot delivers over 600bhp (see page 11), that's almost three times the power of the Bentley engine.

This duct directs air onto the brakes to keep them cool.

The car's body comes off in sections to make it easy for the mechanics to get to the parts they want to repair.

This small piece of glass acts as a windshield for the passenger in the front seat. It is called an aeroscreen, because a similar screen was first used on aircraft.

The driver can flip up this wire mesh screen to protect himself from stones thrown up by cars in front.

Racing in the 1930s

Bentleys were just one of the famous makes of cars that raced in the 1930s. Others included Bugatti, Alfa Romeo and Mercedes-Benz. Racing cars of this time were usually open-topped. To keep warm, clean and dry, drivers wrapped themselves up in many layers of clothes and often a final covering of leather coats, hats, gloves and goggles.

This is a Bentley racing at Le Mans over 60 years ago.

The spare tyre is bolted on to the outside of the car body.

These slots in the car body are called vents. They let air inside the body to cool the engine down.

The leather strap stops the engine cover from flying open.

The Bentleys were originally painted in this distinctive and famous shade of green. It is called British racing green.

This is the Bentley symbol found on all Bentley cars.

The front headlight has a wire mesh cover to stop stones from breaking the glass.

This is the cap which seals in the water used in the car's radiator.

This large, heavy pole is the steering column. It connects the steering wheel to the steering system used to turn the front wheels.

The wheel is held together by spokes like those on a bicycle wheel.

This is the car's horn.

Supercharger

Bentley engine

The Bentley's engine was enormous and powerful for its time. It could produce up to 240*bhp**. The top speed of this car was about 201km/h (125mph).

The supercharger

Many Bentleys have a machine called a supercharger which helps the car go faster. It does this by pumping more air and fuel into the engine. The supercharger can be switched on and off by the driver.

Suspension

A car's suspension makes travelling much more comfortable. The car's wheels bounce up and down over holes and bumps in the road. The suspension system stops the whole car from bouncing around uncontrollably. The suspension also helps the wheels to stay in touch with the ground as much as possible. This improves the car's handling which is how drivers describe how easy a car is to control. There are several types of suspension. Many use a spring like the one shown on the right.

Spring

Damper (see below)

Riding on springs

When a car goes over a bump, the spring compresses, squashing up to absorb the energy of the bump; but it must eventually return to its normal position. A spring expands as quickly as it compresses. It expands past its normal size then is pulled back.

   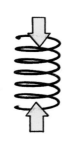

Normal size   Compressed   Expanded   Compressed

Springs rise and fall many times before they get back to normal size. A car body fitted only with springs would bounce up and down for quite some time. The solution is to fit each spring with a device called a damper.

Car body with just springs for suspension.

Car body rises and falls for a long time.

How a damper works

A damper slows the rise of the spring. The most common type of damper uses a piston joined to the spring and a cylinder of oil. This is called a hydraulic damper. It works by using special openings called valves*. Oil travels through these valves faster when the piston moves down the cylinder than when it moves up. This means that the spring can compress quickly but expands slowly.

Cylinder full of oil

Valve

Oil flows faster through valves in this direction.

Piston

Active suspension

This modern system of suspension uses *hydraulic* * cylinders instead of springs and dampers. The height of each wheel is controlled by the cylinders which are connected to a central computer in the car. Active suspension greatly improves a car's handling.

When accelerating, active suspension stops the front wheels from rising off the ground.

When braking sharply, active suspension stops the front of a car from dipping down.

When cornering sharply the inner wheels tend to rise. Active suspension helps keep them on the ground.

You can see the springs and dampers connected to each wheel on this picture.

Car suspension springs have to be strong to cushion the weight of a loaded car as it goes over a bump.

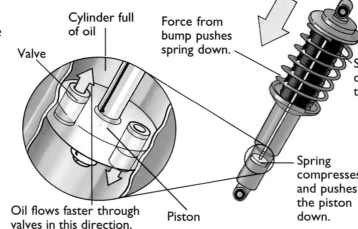

The suspension springs are joined to this car separately from the dampers.

This is the rear *axle*.

Force from bump pushes spring down.

Spring connected to piston.

Spring compresses and pushes the piston down.

As spring rises, it pulls the piston back up the cylinder.

Valves and oil slow the spring's rise.

Steering

Turning a car's steering wheel seems quite easy but your effort has to be increased so that you can turn the heavy car with its wheels gripping the ground strongly. Many cars use a system of two interlocking *gears** called a rack and pinion. At the end of the steering wheel column is the pinion. This interlocks with a sliding, toothed rail called the rack.

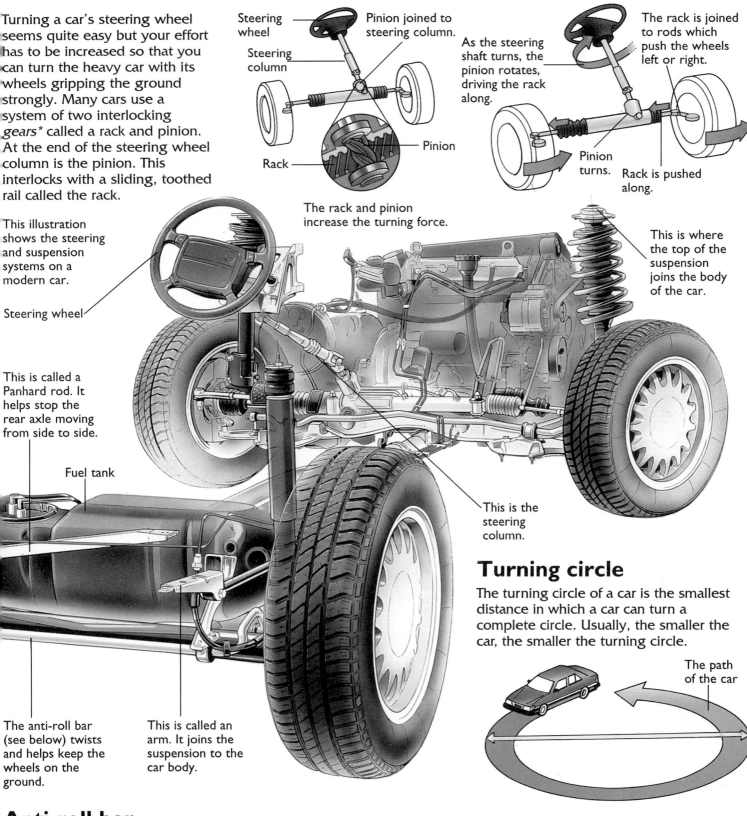

Steering wheel

Pinion joined to steering column.

Steering column

Rack

Pinion

The rack and pinion increase the turning force.

As the steering shaft turns, the pinion rotates, driving the rack along.

The rack is joined to rods which push the wheels left or right.

Pinion turns.

Rack is pushed along.

This is where the top of the suspension joins the body of the car.

This illustration shows the steering and suspension systems on a modern car.

Steering wheel

This is called a Panhard rod. It helps stop the rear axle moving from side to side.

Fuel tank

This is the steering column.

The anti-roll bar (see below) twists and helps keep the wheels on the ground.

This is called an arm. It joins the suspension to the car body.

Turning circle

The turning circle of a car is the smallest distance in which a car can turn a complete circle. Usually, the smaller the car, the smaller the turning circle.

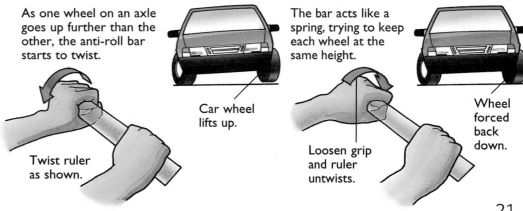

The path of the car

Anti-roll bar

An anti-roll bar is a steel rod connected to the frame of the car. It helps prevent a car from leaning over on tight, fast corners or after hitting a large bump in the road. It does this by stopping the wheel from rising too high in the air. On the right you can see how it works by imitating its movement with a long, plastic ruler.

As one wheel on an axle goes up further than the other, the anti-roll bar starts to twist.

Car wheel lifts up.

Twist ruler as shown.

The bar acts like a spring, trying to keep each wheel at the same height.

Loosen grip and ruler untwists.

Wheel forced back down.

Brakes

Braking is all about stopping wheels that are spinning very fast. A modern car has a brake on each wheel and these all work at the same time when you press the brake lever. There are two main types of brake, disc and drum brakes. Both types use a *hydraulic** system.

Hydraulic system

Modern brakes are powered by a liquid put under pressure, called a *hydraulic** system. With the help of the car engine, the liquid is forced through pipes and cylinders to make the brakes move.

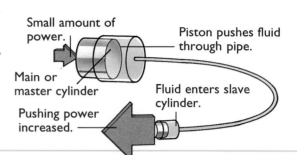

Small amount of power.

Main or master cylinder

Pushing power increased.

Piston pushes fluid through pipe.

Fluid enters slave cylinder.

Disc brakes

Disc brakes are similar to brakes on a bicycle. Bicycle brakes have a lever called a caliper which opens and closes. On the ends of the caliper are brake pads which press hard onto the rim of the bicycle wheel. The *friction**, or rubbing, created by the pads slows the wheel down. When a car disc brake works, hydraulic fluid forces the caliper to close onto a disc joined to the car wheel.

Here you can see where a disc brake fits inside a wheel.

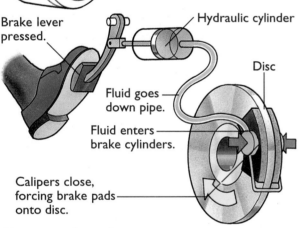

Brake lever pressed.

Hydraulic cylinder

Fluid goes down pipe.

Fluid enters brake cylinders.

Disc

Calipers close, forcing brake pads onto disc.

Here is a car disc brake.

Brake caliper

Brake pads grip the disc very strongly and create much friction.

This clip holds the brake pads in place.

This is the hub of the wheel.

This is one of the brake cylinders.

This disc is joined to the wheel.

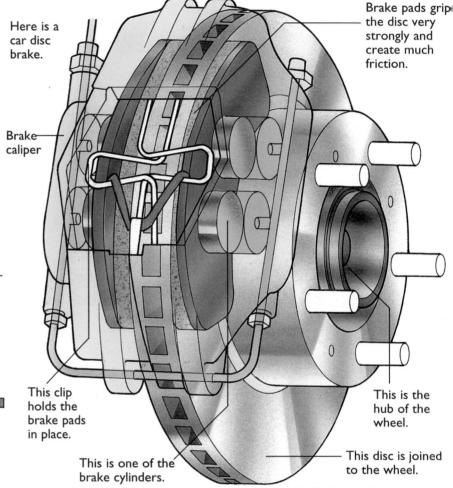

Drum brakes

Drum brakes are so-called because they have a metal drum attached to the car wheel instead of a disc.

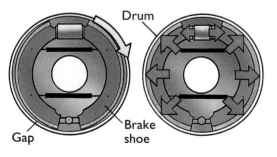

Drum

Gap

Brake shoe

Brake pads fit on curved brake shoes which sit inside the drum. There is a gap between the shoes and drum.

When the driver brakes, a hydraulic system pushes the shoes out to touch the drum. This slows the wheel down.

The inside of a drum brake.

Brake shoe

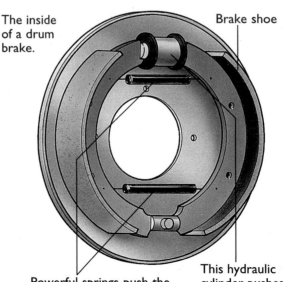

Powerful springs push the shoes away from the drum when the brake is released.

This hydraulic cylinder pushes the brake shoe onto the drum.

ABS braking

Sometimes, if brakes are pressed too hard, they can lock and stop the wheels from spinning. If the wheels are not going around, the driver cannot steer and may skid and hit something. ABS, or anti-locking brake system, has sensors on the wheels linked to a computer. This can adjust the brake pressure up to 10 or 12 times a second. This means the brakes are put on and off a fraction all the time; enough to allow the driver to brake and steer safely around hazards.

Tyres

Modern tyres are complicated car parts, designed by computers and tested as thoroughly as, and sometimes more than, other parts of the car. So much work goes into designing and making them because they are vital to a car's safety and performance. Tyres are the only part of the car that touch the ground. They must be able to grip the road enough to move the car along efficiently and allow the driver to control the car easily both in a straight line or when turning.

This is a modern car tyre, made by Michelin. It is made up of many different layers called plies.

Types of tyre

There are many different types of tyres for different vehicles and driving conditions.

The first tyres were made of solid rubber. This tyre from a Bugatti car of the 1930s is filled with air like a modern one but is not as wide.

This tyre is made for rallying across heavy mud or sand. It has a very deep, chunky tread, a lot like tyres used on tractors.

This tyre is very wide and has almost no tread. It is used by Grand Prix cars when the track is completely dry. If it rains, the tyre must be swapped for one with more tread.

Radial tyres*, like this one, have plies running at right angles to the side walls.

The top surface of a tyre is marked with a pattern of grooves called the tread.

The tread clears water, mud, dirt and snow out from between the tyre and the road.

This layer is called the undertread. It is made of tough rubber.

Tyre rubber is a mixture of natural rubber which can stand a lot of heat and man-made rubber which is more hard wearing.

This part of the tyre is made from thin steel wires all woven together. It makes the tyre stronger.

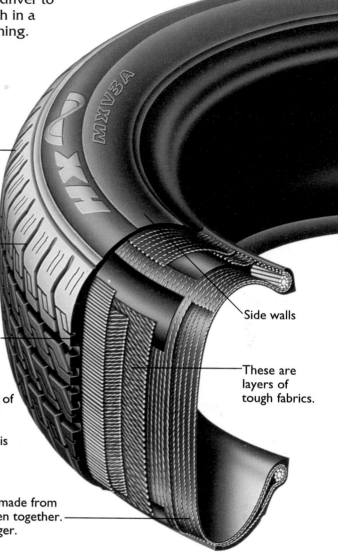

Side walls

These are layers of tough fabrics.

Grip in wet weather

If the grooves in the tread of a tyre are too narrow or too shallow, they cannot do their job properly. Instead of spraying water out from under the tyre so it can grip the road, a slippery film of water forms between the tyre and the road. The car can lose its grip and go out of control. This is called aquaplaning. Modern tread is designed to avoid this.

This new Goodyear tyre has a large channel down its middle to remove more water than an ordinary road tyre.

Complicated tread pattern

This special photo shows water being directed out from under the tyre.

The part of the tyre you can see above is the footprint. That is the part which touches the ground at any one time.

Getting rid of tyres

Millions of worn down tyres go for scrap every year. Because each tyre is made from a range of different materials, they are hard to recycle. Some tyres are burned but many are buried underground where they can create pollution or help fuel dangerous underground fires.

There are other, less harmful ways to dispose of scrap tyres. For example, some can be given a new layer of tread in a complicated process called retreading or remoulding.

These parts of the car bumper are made from scrap tyres.

Sports car

Sports cars are the quickest cars on the road. They can start off very fast and steer precisely and accurately. They are great fun to drive, but are often small inside and extremely expensive to buy. Some drivers race their sports cars on tracks. Famous sports car makers include Ferrari, Lotus, Chevrolet and Jaguar.

The 911 has been changed many times. However, it still looks similar to this early model.

Porsche 911 Carrera 4

First built in 1963, the Porsche 911 is one of the best-known sports cars. It has raced at Le Mans and won the Monte Carlo rally. Over 250,000 have been built. This Carrera 4 model is one of the latest of many versions of the 911.

Here's the spare wheel.

This fan cools the oil used in the engine.

Rounded design

Dr Ferdinand Porsche designed one of the world's most popular cars many years before the Porsche company built the 911. The two cars have a rounded shape. Can you guess what the other car is? Turn to page 32 for the answer.

This car has its fuel tank at the front.

This drive shaft takes power from the engine to the car's wheels.

Four wheel drive

In most cars the engine feeds power either to the back or front pair of wheels. The wheels that do not receive power are pushed or pulled by the others. In a four wheel drive car, all four wheels receive power straight from the engine. This helps the car grip the road better and makes it easier for the driver to control it in bad weather.

The engine's power can be varied between the back and front wheels, depending on which can grip the road better. In normal driving, the back wheels get 70% and the front wheels, 30%.

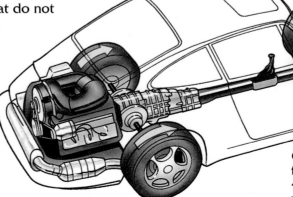

On very icy roads, the Porsche four wheel drive can produce 40% more grip than the two wheel drive version of the car.

Acceleration

Acceleration is how fast a car can increase its speed. Sports cars must have good acceleration. This is often measured as how quickly a car can go from standing still to 100km/h (62mph). The 911 Carrera 4 can do this in 5.7 seconds.

This Porsche 959 can accelerate from 0 to 100km/h (62mph) in 3.9 seconds.

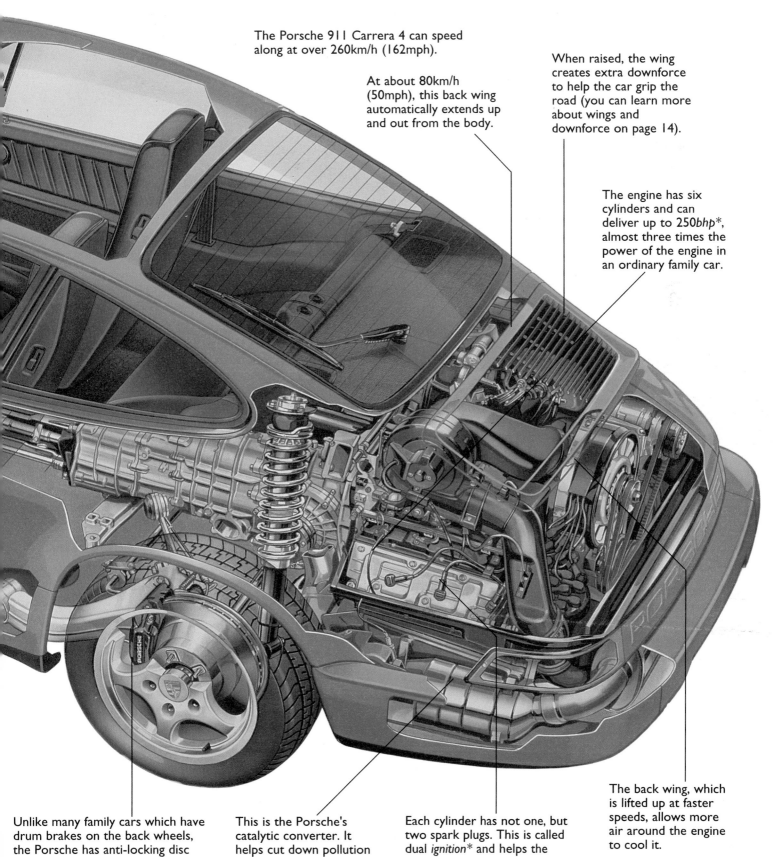

The Porsche 911 Carrera 4 can speed along at over 260km/h (162mph).

At about 80km/h (50mph), this back wing automatically extends up and out from the body.

When raised, the wing creates extra downforce to help the car grip the road (you can learn more about wings and downforce on page 14).

The engine has six cylinders and can deliver up to 250*bhp**, almost three times the power of the engine in an ordinary family car.

Unlike many family cars which have drum brakes on the back wheels, the Porsche has anti-locking disc brakes on all four wheels.

This is the Porsche's catalytic converter. It helps cut down pollution from the engine.

Each cylinder has not one, but two spark plugs. This is called dual *ignition** and helps the engine run more smoothly.

The back wing, which is lifted up at faster speeds, allows more air around the engine to cool it.

25

Electrical system

A modern car would not work without its electrical system. Electricity is needed to start the car, to make the spark plugs burn the air and fuel mixture in the engine and to power the lights, windshield wipers and other electrical parts of the car.

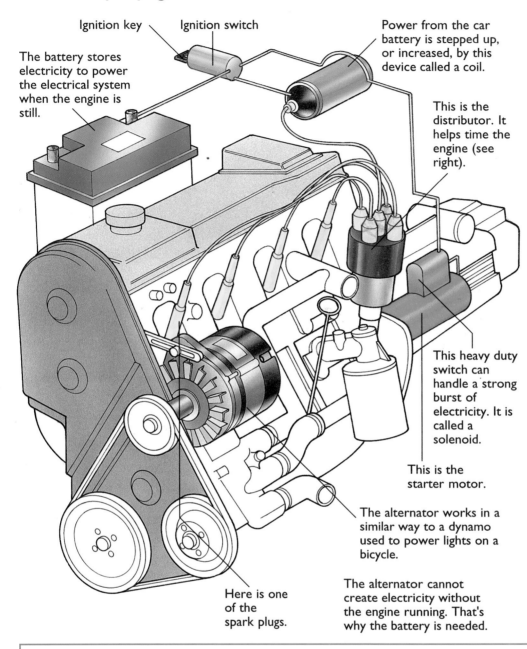

Ignition key

Ignition switch

The battery stores electricity to power the electrical system when the engine is still.

Power from the car battery is stepped up, or increased, by this device called a coil.

This is the distributor. It helps time the engine (see right).

This heavy duty switch can handle a strong burst of electricity. It is called a solenoid.

This is the starter motor.

The alternator works in a similar way to a dynamo used to power lights on a bicycle.

The alternator cannot create electricity without the engine running. That's why the battery is needed.

Here is one of the spark plugs.

Starting the engine

Turning the ignition key releases electricity from the battery, which passes through the solenoid switch to the starter motor.

The starter motor turns the engine's flywheel making the pistons move up and down the cylinders. At the same time, more electricity is passed to the coil.

The coil increases the electricity's voltage. The electricity is then fed to the distributor which times the electricity reaching the spark plugs.

As the engine runs, it turns the alternator. The alternator uses this movement to create electricity, which it feeds to the battery and uses to run the electrical system.

The spark plugs start producing sparks which set light to the air and fuel mixture in the cylinder.

Lights

Lights are needed for driving in fog, bad weather conditions and at night. All modern cars have many different lights but they were considered luxury accessories until the 1930s. The first lights were powered by gas like old street lamps but today, all car lights are powered by electricity.

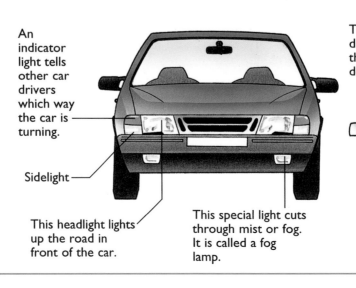

An indicator light tells other car drivers which way the car is turning.

Sidelight

This headlight lights up the road in front of the car.

This special light cuts through mist or fog. It is called a fog lamp.

These brake lights tell drivers behind that the car is slowing down.

Some new cars ha extra brake lights the rear window.

Reversing light

Rear indicator lights

Timing the engine

The power from the coil has to reach the spark plugs at precisely the right time. If it doesn't, then the engine will run very poorly. Getting the timing right is the job of the distributor.

At the middle of the distributor is an arm which turns at a speed decided by how fast the engine is working. Each time the arm gets close to a metal point, it completes an electrical circuit which passes electricity on to the spark plug.

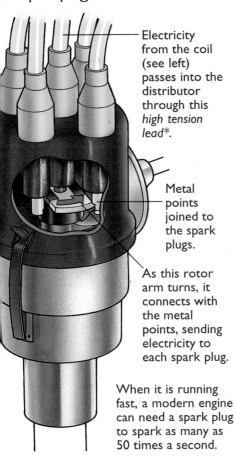

Electricity from the coil (see left) passes into the distributor through this *high tension lead**.

Metal points joined to the spark plugs.

As this rotor arm turns, it connects with the metal points, sending electricity to each spark plug.

When it is running fast, a modern engine can need a spark plug to spark as many as 50 times a second.

The car's instruments

The dashboard is the panel in front of the driver and it holds many of the instruments and controls used to drive a car. Some cars now have a screen which displays maps of where the car is heading. The screen is joined to a navigation computer which can offer suggested routes between two places. Nearly all cars have heaters and air fans to keep the driver and passengers at a comfortable temperature.

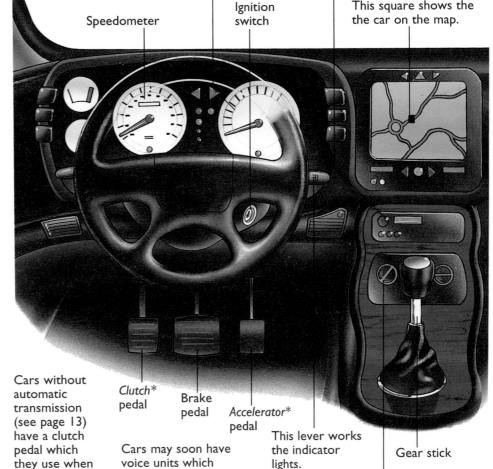

Rev counter. This tells the driver how many revolutions, or turns, the engine's crankshaft makes every minute.

The latest car radios pick up radio traffic reports which can warn of dangerous roads, traffic jams and so on.

Ignition switch

This square shows the the car on the map.

Speedometer

Cars without automatic transmission (see page 13) have a clutch pedal which they use when changing gears.

Clutch* pedal

Brake pedal

Cars may soon have voice units which offer advice on which way to go.

Accelerator* pedal

This lever works the indicator lights.

Gear stick

Passenger compartment heater controls.

Dipping headlights

Most countries have rules about the number, type and position of lights on a car. One of the most important rules is about dipping headlights. Full headlights are used when there are no other vehicles on the road. Bright headlights pointing straight ahead, however, can dazzle the driver of a car coming the other way. To prevent this, modern headlights are designed to dip their beam down onto the road at the flick of a switch.

Dipped lights

Full lights

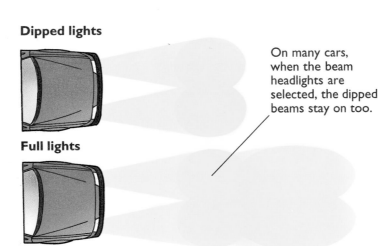

On many cars, when the beam headlights are selected, the dipped beams stay on too.

This sports car has odd pop up lights. Do you know why? (see page 32 for the answer).

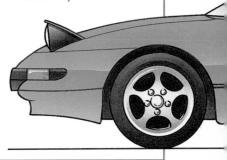

Off-road car

Cars are sometimes needed off roads to drive over rough ground. Off-road cars are as happy on the road as they are over grassland or on a bumpy dirt track.

Range Rover LSE

The Range Rover is a very popular off-road vehicle made by the Land Rover company. The LSE version shown here has a top speed of 180km/h (112mph) and weighs 2150kg (4740lb) when it is empty.

The roof is specially strengthened just in case the car rolls over.

Most off-road vehicles, including the Range Rover, have four wheel drive. See page 24 to learn more about it.

The engine can produce up to 200*bhp**. It has eight cylinders arranged in a V-shaped pattern called a V8.

This Range Rover has an automatic gearbox.

This steel loop can be used as a towbar if the car gets really stuck somewhere and needs to be pulled out.

This air suspension unit replaces the coiled spring in a normal suspension system (see right).

This is the damper for the front left wheel.

This piece of bodywork is called the wheel arch.

The Range Rover in action

The police use the car for traffic control.

Off-road vehicles like the Range Rover are used for all sorts of jobs. Many police forces in Great Britain and abroad have Range Rovers. It is used as an ambulance and fire-fighting vehicle in some isolated areas. Farmers and forestry workers use the Range Rover for travelling through deep, muddy streams and over very rough ground.

Range Rovers can cross deep streams.

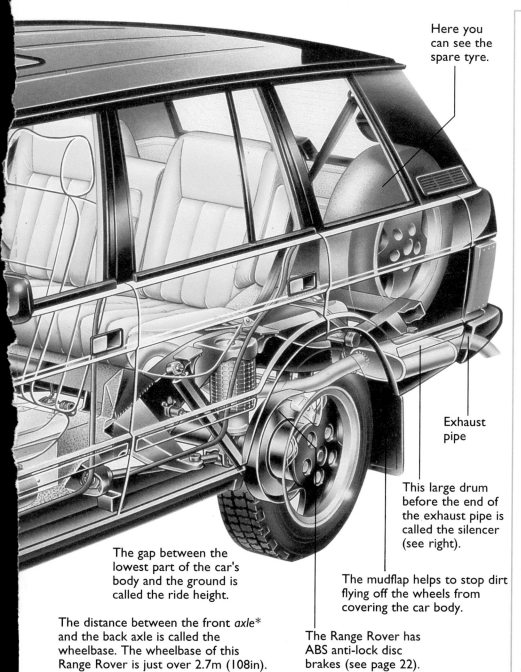

Here you can see the spare tyre.

The gap between the lowest part of the car's body and the ground is called the ride height.

The distance between the front *axle** and the back axle is called the wheelbase. The wheelbase of this Range Rover is just over 2.7m (108in).

Exhaust pipe

This large drum before the end of the exhaust pipe is called the silencer (see right).

The mudflap helps to stop dirt flying off the wheels from covering the car body.

The Range Rover has ABS anti-lock disc brakes (see page 22).

Air suspension

The Range Rover's suspension system uses powerful dampers and anti-roll bars, but it doesn't use normal springs (see page 20). Instead, *pneumatic** cylinders, full of pressurized air, are used to cushion the car body and absorb much of the energy from a bump or rut.

The suspension units on each wheel are independent. This means that each wheel can adjust its positioning as the car travels over uneven surfaces. Electronic sensors linked to a computer inside the car can adjust the gap between the car body and the wheels.

To clear obstructions, the body can rise up off the wheels.

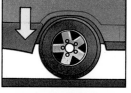

For loading and unloading, the car body drops low over the wheels.

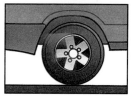

When going fast, the car lowers to improve its aerodynamics (see pages 16-17).

The exhaust system

The waste gases from the engine are piped out of the car by the exhaust system. As they leave the engine they are very hot and at a high pressure which would make a lot of noise if they went straight into the air. The exhaust system forces the gases on a long journey through pipes and a special device called a silencer (or muffler). By the time the gases leave the exhaust system they are much cooler and quieter.

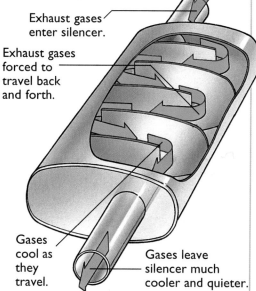

Exhaust gases enter silencer.

Exhaust gases forced to travel back and forth.

Gases cool as they travel.

Gases leave silencer much cooler and quieter.

Catalytic converter

The waste gases from the exhaust contain many substances which pollute the air. Many cars now use lead-free petrol as lead is a serious pollutant. More and more cars are also being fitted with a catalytic converter. This changes some of the waste gases that pass through it into other, less harmful chemicals. For example, dangerous nitrogen oxides are converted into harmless nitrogen and water.

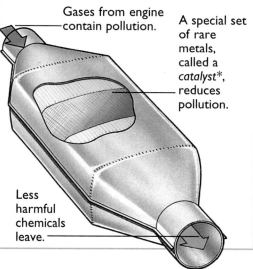

Gases from engine contain pollution.

A special set of rare metals, called a *catalyst**, reduces pollution.

Less harmful chemicals leave.

The future

Cars in the future will still need brakes, steering, suspension and all the other systems shown in this book. With the exception of a few top sports cars, future cars will not go much faster. But they are expected to be safer, easier to drive and less harmful to the environment. Here is a possible car of tomorrow with some of the futuristic features that it may include.

This car would be built using highly advanced robots and computers. These would cut down the amount of materials wasted in building a car.

Complex electronics mean that the engine uses less fuel and produces less pollution. If a car uses 10% less fuel, it will use about 1500 litres (330 gallons) less in its whole lifetime.

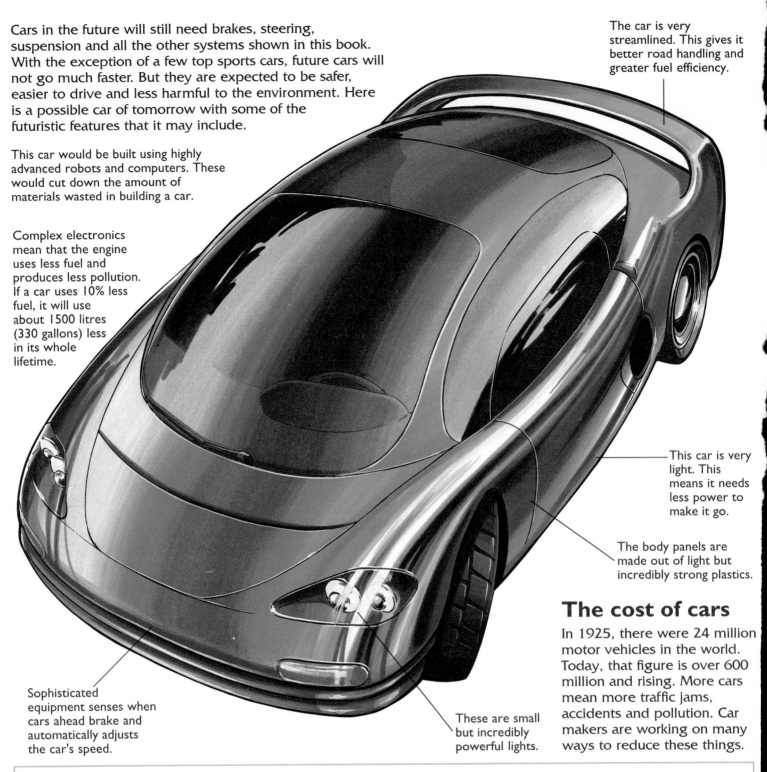

The car is very streamlined. This gives it better road handling and greater fuel efficiency.

This car is very light. This means it needs less power to make it go.

The body panels are made out of light but incredibly strong plastics.

Sophisticated equipment senses when cars ahead brake and automatically adjusts the car's speed.

These are small but incredibly powerful lights.

The cost of cars

In 1925, there were 24 million motor vehicles in the world. Today, that figure is over 600 million and rising. More cars mean more traffic jams, accidents and pollution. Car makers are working on many ways to reduce these things.

Safety

Safety researchers will find new ways to protect passengers in a crash. In fact, experts expect to find many new ways to prevent accidents in the first place.

Sensors will be able to scan the road ahead much better than a driver's eyes, especially in the dark and fog. Information from the cameras will appear on instruments called Head Up Displays (HUDs). The driver can see these without bending his head to look. At the moment, HUDs are only found in modern fighter jets.

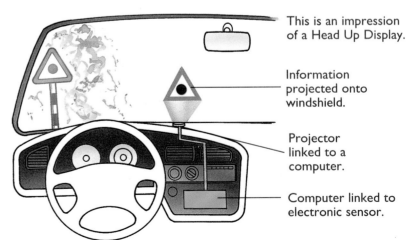

This is an impression of a Head Up Display.

Information projected onto windshield.

Projector linked to a computer.

Computer linked to electronic sensor.

Design your own

Virtual reality machines, which can show you exactly how it would look and feel inside your car, may allow you to design the interior to your own taste before the car is built.

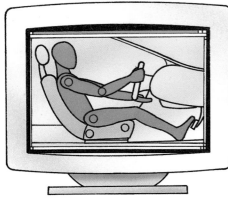

This dummy on the computer screen is testing the driver's seat. The dummy can be altered to the size of each car buyer.

Electric power

Electric cars, such as the one on page 11, are likely to become more common. Many will use a powerful battery which can be recharged, but some may be solar-powered like this three-wheeled car. It was built in Japan and called the Honda Dream.

Solar panels

It averaged a speed of 85km/h (53mph) when it won an Australian race for solar cars.

City driving

Special small cars for crowded towns and cities will become popular. Below is a city car being built by Ford. In the years ahead, similar-shaped cars may be powered by a small electric motor, have solar panels on their roof and be able to park themselves automatically without any help from the driver.

This is Ford's prototype of a city car, the Ka.

Glossary

Accelerator. The pedal that controls the speed of the engine and, so, the speed of the car.

Aerodynamics. The science of how gases, such as air, move over an object. Aerodynamics affects the way cars are designed and built.

Air pressure. The force with which air pushes against an object. Air pressure is increased by pushing air into a small space. This is called compressing.

Alternator. A device which generates electricity from the engine's movement.

Axle. The bar or rod on which the car's wheels turn.

Brake horsepower (bhp). One common measure of the power produced by an engine. It is used by many car manufacturers in their advertisements.

Cam. A small, usually oval, wheel which helps to convert turning movement into up and down movement.

Catalyst. A substance which changes how other chemicals react. A catalyst in a car's exhaust system is used to lower pollution.

Chassis. The framework of the car, usually made of steel. Most of the car's main parts, such as the engine and body panels, are attached to it.

Clutch. Operated by a pedal, it disconnects the gearbox from the engine long enough for the gear to be changed smoothly.

Crank. Something that helps to convert up and down movement into turning movement.

Cross ply tyres. Tyres with their plies running diagonally across in overlapping layers.

Differential. A set of gears that allow the car's wheels to turn at different speeds when the vehicle goes around a corner.

Distributor. A part of the engine which makes the spark plugs produce a spark at precisely the right time.

Fan belt. A belt which is powered by the engine and helps power the alternator and the engine cooling fan.

Firing order. The order in which the spark plugs produce sparks.

Fossil fuel. Fuels formed by dead plants and animals squashed together over millions of years in the same way that fossils are created. Coal and oil are examples of fossil fuels.

Friction. The resistance found when one surface moves and rubs against another surface.

Gears. Devices with grooves or teeth on their edges that mesh, or link, with each other. When they are powered they can turn each other around. Many gears are toothed wheels like those that drive a bicycle chain.

Handbrake. A hand-operated lever usually connected to the back brakes. It holds a car still when parked.

High tension lead. A thick lead which carries high voltage electricity to and from certain parts of the engine, such as between the distributor and the spark plugs.

Hydraulics. Using a liquid to transmit power from one place to another. A car's brake system uses hydraulics. Early hydraulic machines used water but most today use oil or other liquids that do not freeze as easily as water.

Ignition. Setting light to and burning the fuel and air mixture in the engine's cylinders.

Lubricant. A slippery liquid, such as oil, used to cover surfaces that rub together. The lubricant helps reduce friction.The process of using a liquid in this way is called lubrication.

Pneumatic. Using a compressed gas, usually air, to fill a container or transmit power.

Radial tyres. Tyres which have their layers or plies running across the tyre at a right angle to the rim of the wheel.

Streamlining. To shape a car's body so that it can move through the air as smoothly as possible.

Tachometer. This is also known as the rev. counter. It shows the engine's speed in the form of how many times the crankshaft turns around every minute.

Torque. The turning force from an engine.

Tuning. Adjusting the car's engine so that it performs at its best.

Valve. A device that acts like a door, opening, closing and controlling the flow of a liquid or gas through a pipe or tube.

Volume. The measurement of how much space an object takes up.

Wheel spin. When the car's tyres cannot grip the road properly. This often happens when the road is slippery or icy or when the tyres are in very poor condition.

Index

Answers to questions

Page 24
Dr Ferdinand Porsche designed the famous Volkswagen Beetle before he designed the Porsche 911.

Page 27
The sports car's front lights pop up so that they are high enough off the ground to give a good beam and be clearly seen by other cars. When the lights are not being used, they pop down into the body making the car more *streamlined**.

No part of this publication may be reproduced in whole or in part, or stored in a retrieval system, or transmitted in any form or by any means, electronic, mechanical, photocopying, recording, or otherwise, without written permission of the publisher. For information regarding permission, write to Usborne Publishing Ltd., Usborne House, 83-85 Saffron Hill, London EC1N 8RT, England.

ISBN 0-590-62395-8

Copyright © 1994 by Usborne Publishing Ltd. First published in Great Britain in 1994 by Usborne Publishing Ltd. All rights reserved. Published by Scholastic Inc., 555 Broadway, New York, NY 10012, by arrangement with Usborne Publishing Ltd.

12 11 10 9 8 7 6 5 4 3 2 1   6 7 8 9/9 0/0

Printed in the U.S.A.   08
First Scholastic printing, September 1995